The User's Journey

How the mind works through texts and design

Copyright ®

All copyrights for this content are reserved. No part of this text may be reproduced, stored or transmitted in any form or by any means, electronic, mechanical, photocopying, recording or otherwise, without the prior written permission of the copyright holder.

Any unauthorized use of this content constitutes copyright infringement and subjects the violator to legal action. All texts, images and other material contained in this content are the property of the copyright holder, unless otherwise indicated.

The copyright holder reserves the right to make changes, corrections and updates to this content at any time and without notice. Use of this content is strictly for informational and educational purposes and should not be construed as legal or professional advice.

The user's mind plays a crucial role when experimenting with texts and design, and its workings can be analyzed from a scientific perspective. Let's explore some key aspects of this process.

When a user interacts with a text or design, various cognitive activities take place in their mind. At the perceptual level, visual and textual stimuli are processed by sensory systems such as vision and reading. The user's mind interprets and analyzes visual elements such as colors, shapes, images and typography, as well as the structure and content of the text.

Understanding the text involves activating linguistic processes, such as decoding words, attributing meaning and interpreting sentences. Users use their prior knowledge, vocabulary, and experiences to understand the messages conveyed by the text.

They also assess the clarity, cohesion and coherence of the text, seeking to obtain a complete and coherent meaning.

As for design, the user's mind processes visual information holistically, identifying patterns, hierarchies and structures. Design principles such as contrast, alignment, proximity, and balance influence the perception and visual organization of information. Users also apply mindsets and expectations based on their past experiences to interpret and navigate the design.

Furthermore, the user's mind is influenced by emotional and motivational factors when experimenting with texts and design. Emotions play an important role in forming attitudes and in the affective response to experiences. Users may experience positive feelings such as satisfaction and pleasure, or negative feelings such as frustration and confusion, depending on the quality and appropriateness of the text and design.

The cognitive and emotional processes of the user's mind are studied by several scientific disciplines, such as cognitive psychology, experimental psychology and neuroscience. These studies provide valuable insights into how users perceive, understand, evaluate and respond to texts and designs, enabling UX and design professionals to make informed decisions and create more effective and engaging experiences.

Ultimately, you'll see that the user's mind plays a complex and multifaceted role when experimenting with text and design. Perceptual processing, textual comprehension, visual perception, emotions and motivation are some of the aspects involved in this process. Understanding these mechanisms scientifically helps create more impactful and meaningful experiences for users.

A brief introduction to the UX world

User Experience (UX) is a discipline that seeks to understand and improve the interaction between users and a product, system or service.

This area of study is fundamental to create satisfactory, intuitive and efficient experiences, taking into account the needs, desires and expectations of users. In this text, we will explore the concept of UX, its importance and origin.

The emergence of the term "User Experience" dates back to the 1990s, when researcher Don Norman popularized the concept in his work "The Design of Everyday Things".

Norman was one of the pioneering figures in the field of cognitive ergonomics and championed the importance of designing user-centered products.

However, it is important to highlight that the concept of UX was not invented by a single person, but evolved from several interdisciplinary fields, such as psychology, ergonomics, interaction design and cognitive science.

The idea that the user experience is essential for the success of a product began to gain prominence as technology became increasingly present in people's daily lives.

The advent of the internet and the exponential growth of digital applications boosted the need to create friendlier and more accessible interfaces. In this context, UX has come to be recognized as a competitive advantage for companies, since user satisfaction and loyalty have become essential elements for the success of a product or service.

In the beginning, the focus was mainly on usability, that is, on ensuring that the products were easy to use and met the needs of users.

Over time, the concept of UX expanded beyond usability, also considering emotional, affective and aesthetic aspects of the user experience.

The field of UX covers a wide range of activities and methodologies. One of the fundamental steps is user research, which involves collecting information about users' needs, desires, expectations and behaviors. This research can be carried out through interviews, questionnaires, observations or other methods, allowing UX professionals to better understand the target audience and their contexts of use.

Based on the insights gained through user research, UX professionals develop personas, which are fictional representations of users with similar characteristics and needs.

Personas help guide the design process, allowing designers to step into users' shoes and make decisions based on their perspectives.

In the UX process, it is also important to create wireframes and prototypes. Wireframes are sketches or visual schematics that represent the structure and layout of an interface. Prototypes are interactive versions of the product that allow testing and validating concepts, functionalities and interaction flows with users before full development.

Information architecture is another field that plays a key role in UX.

It focuses on the organization, structure, and navigation of information in a product or system. A well-planned information architecture makes it easier to find and understand information, making the user experience more efficient and satisfying.

Next to it, we have interface design, which is another essential area in the UX field. It involves the visual and interactive creation of interface elements, such as buttons, menus, icons and colors. A good interface design seeks harmony between aesthetics and functionality, ensuring that the interface is attractive, intuitive and easy to use.

In addition to research, prototyping, information architecture and interface design, UX also encompasses usability evaluation and testing. These activities make it possible to identify problems and opportunities for improvement in the user's interaction with the product. Through testing with real users, you can get valuable feedback and make necessary adjustments to ensure a more satisfying user experience.

Importantly, UX is not just limited to digital products, but also applies to physical products and services. From the packaging of a product to the service experience in a brick-and-mortar store, UX encompasses every interaction a user has with a brand or organization.

The application of UX brings a series of benefits for both companies and users. For companies, a good UX can result in greater customer satisfaction, increased loyalty, greater competitiveness in the market and even reduced costs related to support and training. For users, a well-designed UX means ease of use, efficiency, pleasure in interaction, and fulfillment of their needs.

In recent years, UX has become increasingly valued and integrated into product and service development practices. Companies from different industries are investing in UX teams, recognizing their strategic importance and impact on business results.

Finally, User Experience (UX) is a discipline that aims to improve the interaction between users and products, systems or services. It emerged as a response to the need to design positive and meaningful experiences for users, taking into account their needs, desires and expectations. Through a user-centric approach, UX seeks to create products and services that are easy to use, efficient, pleasant and that meet the needs of users. With the growing importance of design and user experience, the field of UX continues to evolve, driven by constant technological innovation and the demand for increasingly intuitive and satisfying products and services.

The 5 fundamental pillars of usability

Imagine that you are organizing a special dinner for your friends.

To ensure that everyone has a pleasant experience, you need to consider five fundamental aspects: the diversity of tastes and preferences, the efficiency in preparing dishes, the ability to memorize recipes, the prevention of culinary errors and, of course, customer satisfaction. guests.

First, you need to take into account the diversity of tastes and preferences. As with UX design, it's important to offer options that meet the different needs of your guests, such as vegetarian, gluten-free dishes or dishes with specific dietary restrictions. This will ensure that everyone can enjoy dinner according to their individual preferences.

Next, efficiency in preparing the dishes is essential. You need to organize your kitchen in such a way as to have the necessary ingredients and utensils within reach, optimizing time and avoiding delays in the delivery of meals. As with UX design, efficiency is crucial for guests to have a smooth experience without unnecessary delays.

Another important aspect is the ability to memorize recipes. Imagine that you need to consult a cookbook at all times to remember the preparation steps. This could cause confusion and wear and tear during dinner. Likewise, in UX design, it is necessary to create an experience that is memorable for users, so that they can interact with the product or service without difficulties, even after a period of absence.

Furthermore, it is crucial to prevent culinary mistakes. Imagine serving a dish that is too salty or leaving out an essential ingredient. This can compromise your guests' experience. In UX design, it is also necessary to think about how to avoid errors that can frustrate users, whether through clear and visual feedback, confirmations of important actions or restrictions that prevent unwanted actions.

Ultimately, guest satisfaction is the ultimate goal. You want them to feel satisfied, enjoy the food, and leave the dinner feeling positive. Likewise, in UX design, user satisfaction is key. The aim is to create an experience that is pleasant, functional and that meets the expectations of users, so that they are satisfied and have a positive perception of the product or service.

This analogy with a special dinner simply illustrates the five pillars of usability, highlighting the importance of considering diversity, efficiency, memorability, error prevention and user satisfaction in any UX design project, but now, get to know each one of them in isolation.

Learning:

Learning refers to the ease with which users can learn to use a product or service. Good UX design should allow users to quickly understand how to interact with the product, without the need for complex instructions. This includes an intuitive interface, with clear and self-explanatory design elements, visual feedback and brief instructions when needed. By prioritizing learning, UX designers seek to minimize the learning curve, so that users can start using the product effectively and autonomously.

Efficiency:

Efficiency refers to how quickly and easily users can accomplish their tasks and achieve their goals when using a product or service. Good UX design aims to optimize workflow and interaction, reducing the effort and time required to complete tasks. This involves simplifying processes, eliminating unnecessary steps, taking shortcuts and automating whenever possible. By prioritizing efficiency, UX designers seek to make the user experience more agile and productive, increasing productivity and minimizing frustrations.

***memorability*:**

Memorability concerns the ease with which users can remember how to use a product or service after a period of time without using it. A good UX design seeks to create an experience that is memorable, so that users can return to the product after a while and resume interaction without difficulty. This can be achieved through consistent visual elements, recognizable design patterns, intuitive navigation structure and a coherent visual language. By prioritizing memorability, UX designers seek to ensure that users can feel comfortable and confident when resuming product use after a lapse of time.

***error prevention*:**

Error prevention refers to the ability of a UX design to avoid or minimize errors made by users. A good UX design should be designed in such a way as to reduce the possibility of errors, making the interaction safer and free of mistakes. This can involve using clear visual feedback, preemptive warnings, confirmations of important actions, and smart restrictions. By prioritizing error prevention, UX designers seek to avoid frustrating situations and improve user confidence by creating an environment where errors are less likely and their impacts are minimized.

User satisfaction:

User satisfaction is a fundamental pillar of UX, referring to the overall experience and positive feeling users have when using a product or service. A good UX design should take into account the emotions and emotional needs of users, creating a pleasant and satisfying experience. This involves design aesthetics, choosing attractive colors and visuals, customizing user preferences, and approaching interactions empathetically. By prioritizing user satisfaction, UX designers seek to create an emotional connection between the user and the product, making the experience memorable and positive.

Each of these fundamental usability pillars is important in its own right, but they are also interconnected and influence each other. For example, a design that prioritizes learning facilitates efficiency, as users who quickly understand how to use the product are able to perform their tasks more quickly. Likewise, a design that prevents errors contributes to user satisfaction, since users frustrated by constant errors will have a negative and unsatisfactory experience.

It is important to highlight that these usability pillars are general guidelines and may vary depending on the context and characteristics of the product or service in question. For example, in a photo editing application, efficiency can be a key factor, allowing users to edit their images quickly and accurately. On a news site, however, learning and memorability may be more relevant, as users must be able to easily find and access the desired information on future visits.

When creating a UX design, it is essential to consider these usability pillars together and balance them according to the users' needs and the goals of the product or service. Each of these pillars plays an important role in creating a successful user experience that is enjoyable, efficient, error-free, and memorable.

The five fundamental pillars of UX usability - learning, efficiency, memorability, error prevention and user satisfaction - are key elements to creating a positive and meaningful user experience.

These pillars guide the design process, helping UX professionals design products and services that are easy to learn, efficient to use, memorable, error-free, and capable of providing a satisfying and enjoyable experience for users. By prioritizing these pillars, companies can increase user satisfaction, brand loyalty and the success of their products or services in the market.

Nielsen's 10 Heuristics

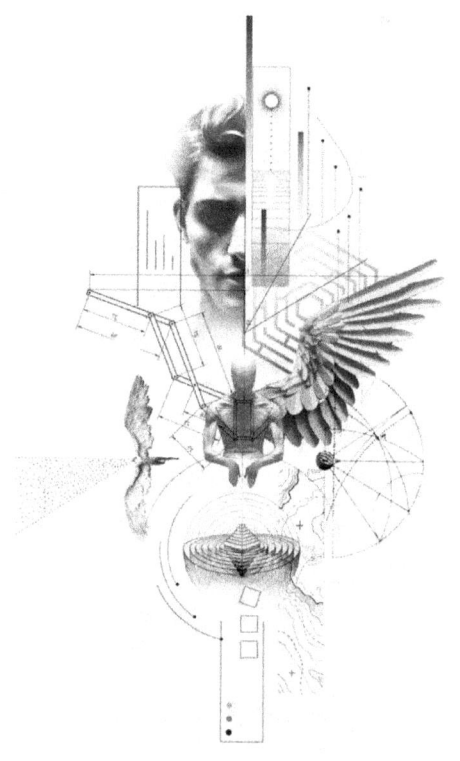

Nielsen's 10 heuristics, also known as "Nielsen's 10 usability heuristics", were proposed by Jakob Nielsen, a renowned usability expert, as a set of guiding principles for evaluating the usability of user interfaces. These heuristics serve as guidelines to identify usability issues in a design and guide necessary improvements. We detail each of them below:

Visibility of system status: The system should always clearly inform users what is happening, whether through visual feedback, status messages or progress indicators. Users must be able to understand what is going on and whether the system is working properly.

Correspondence between the system and the real world: the system should use terminology, concepts and conventions familiar to users, in order to make the interaction more intuitive. Design language and elements should reflect the real world, avoiding complex technical terms or confusing icons.

User control and freedom: Users should have control over their actions and the ability to undo unwanted actions. It is important to provide clearly visible exit options, such as cancel or back buttons, so that users can feel more confident and secure when exploring the system.

Consistency and standards: Design elements should be consistent across the system, following standards recognizable by users. This includes visual, language, and interaction consistency. Standardization facilitates learning and using the system, as users can apply prior knowledge to different parts of the interface.

Error prevention: the system must be designed in such a way as to avoid errors, either through intelligent restrictions, confirmations of important actions or clear and preventive feedback. Users must be guided to avoid actions that could result in unintended consequences or irreversible errors.

Recognition rather than recall: The system should minimize the cognitive load on users by presenting important information clearly and providing hints or reminders whenever necessary. Rather than requiring users to remember specific information, the design should allow for recognition and retrieval of relevant information.

Flexibility and efficiency of use: the system must be designed to serve both novice and experienced users. You should provide shortcuts, advanced functionality, and other options that allow users to perform tasks quickly and efficiently if they wish.

Aesthetics and minimalist design: The interface design should be aesthetically pleasing, with clean and uncluttered visual elements. Too much information or unnecessary elements can distract users and make it difficult to understand. It is important to aim for simplicity and visual clarity.

Help and documentation: the system must provide adequate help and documentation to guide users in case of doubts or difficulties. It is important to offer clear, accessible and relevant information that is available when users need it. However, the design must be intuitive enough that users do not rely exclusively on documentation to use the system.

Error Messages: When errors occur, the system should display clear, precise, and easy-to-understand error messages. Messages should indicate what the problem was and provide guidance on how to fix it. It's important to avoid technical or generic messages that don't help users solve their problems.

These Nielsen heuristics have been widely used as a guide to evaluate the usability of user interfaces in different contexts, from mobile applications to websites and software. By applying these heuristics to a design or evaluation process, UX professionals can identify common issues and target specific improvements to make the user experience more efficient, intuitive, and satisfying.

It is noteworthy that these heuristics are not rigid rules, but general guidelines that can be adapted to the specific needs of each project.

They provide a solid foundation for user-centered design and help create interfaces that are easier to use and meet user expectations.

O Mindset do UX

The UX Mindset, or UX mindset, is an essential approach for professionals working in the User Experience area. It is a way of thinking and acting that places the user at the center of the design process and constantly seeks to understand their needs, desires and expectations.

First, the UX Mindset requires empathy. It is essential to put yourself in the user's shoes, understand their motivations, frustrations and goals. This involves active listening, research, interviews and testing with real users to gain valuable insights to guide design. By adopting empathy, UX professionals are able to create solutions that meet the real needs of users, providing a meaningful and satisfying experience.

In addition to empathy, the UX Mindset requires a continuous learning mindset. The UX area is constantly evolving, and it's important to be open to new ideas, concepts and technologies.

UX professionals must be willing to acquire new knowledge, update themselves on market trends and constantly improve their skills. This learning mindset allows you to keep up with changes in user behavior and best design practices, always seeking to offer innovative and effective solutions.

Another important aspect of the UX Mindset is collaboration. Teamwork is essential for successful UX projects. UX professionals must be willing to collaborate with other team members such as designers, developers, business analysts and stakeholders. Through collaboration, it is possible to integrate different perspectives, share knowledge and create more complete solutions that are in line with the project's objectives. Brainstorming and co-creation help to avoid silos and ensure that everyone involved is aligned with the vision of delivering a great user experience.

Flexibility is also an important feature of the UX Mindset. UX professionals must be open to adapting to different situations, dealing with scope changes and experimenting with new approaches. The first solution is not always the best, and you need to be willing to continually iterate, test, and refine your design based on user feedback and results. Flexibility allows UX professionals to be agile and responsive, ensuring that solutions are truly effective and relevant to users.

Finally, the UX Mindset requires a problem-solving mindset. UX professionals must be curious, analytical and persistent in the search for solutions that meet the challenges presented. They must be able to identify problems, conduct research, analyze data, prototype and test solutions in order to solve the difficulties faced by users. This problem-solving mindset allows UX professionals to be agents of change, driving continuous improvement of the user experience.

In summary, the UX Mindset is a mindset that embraces empathy, continuous learning, collaboration, flexibility and problem solving. By adopting this mindset, UX professionals become user advocates, constantly striving for excellence in creating user-centric products and services.

This approach is not just limited to UX professionals, but can be applied by anyone involved in the process of designing, developing or managing products. The UX Mindset encourages an organizational culture focused on user satisfaction, promoting innovation, quality and product success.

Architecting the information

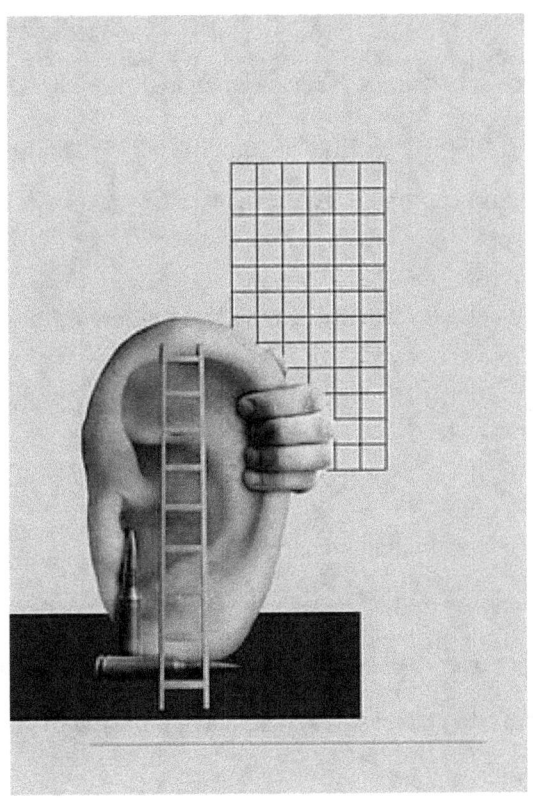

Information architecture is an information design discipline that focuses on organizing, structuring, and presenting information in a clear and understandable way.

It involves creating organization and navigation systems that allow users to find, understand, and interact efficiently with information.

In essence, information architecture has as its main objective to facilitate access and understanding of information, ensuring a satisfactory user experience. It seeks to organize the contents in a logical and coherent way, considering the needs and contexts of the users.

It covers different aspects, such as structuring content, creating categories and classifications, defining navigation systems, creating site maps, and creating taxonomies.

Each of these elements plays a key role in the organization and accessibility of information.

Content structuring involves organizing information hierarchically and sequentially, determining the relationship between different elements and the way they are presented. This includes defining sections, subsections, pages and individual elements such as text, images and videos.

The creation of categories and classifications aims to group elements according to their characteristics and relationships. This categorization can be based on different criteria, such as theme, type of content, target audience, among others. It helps organize information and create more efficient search and navigation systems.

Navigation systems are responsible for providing users with ways to move around and explore information in an intuitive way. This can include menus, links, buttons and other interactive elements that allow users to move between different parts of the information system.

Sitemaps are visual representations of the structure of the information system, providing an overview of available sections and pages. They help users understand the organization of content and quickly find what they are looking for.

It is also related to the usability and accessibility of information, seeking to ensure that information is displayed in a clear, legible and understandable manner, taking into account the characteristics of users and their needs.

In short, information architecture is responsible for creating organizational structures and systems that make information accessible, understandable, and usable by users. It plays a key role in designing interfaces and creating efficient and satisfying user experiences. By applying information architecture principles, UX professionals can ensure that users find information easily and quickly, increasing usability and the overall quality of the user experience.

Know your user

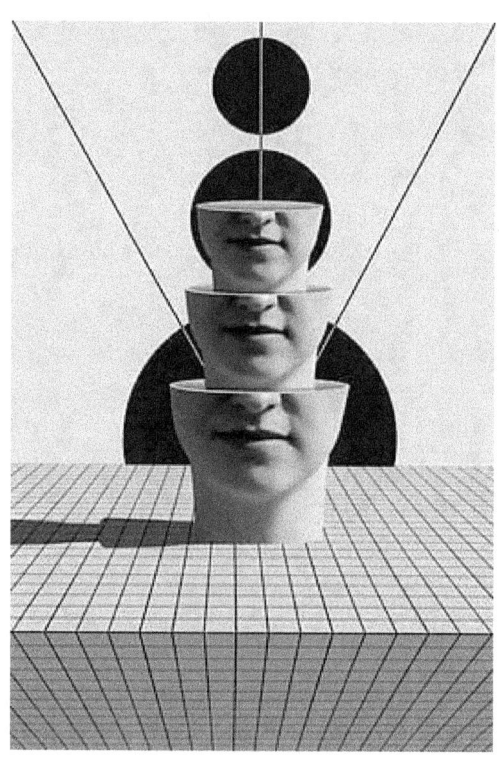

Let's face it: you are not your own user. So you can't just guess what he wants, how he behaves, what his expectations are or what he really thinks about your product.

If you insist on following what YOU THINK is best for your user, you run the risk of making big mistakes. This means you'll be wasting time (yours and your team's) and money investing in tools or adaptations that may simply not work.

Now, to convince you that knowing your user well is essential, here are 4 solid reasons:

Improve product development: It's obvious, but we can't forget it. You can only create an interesting product and improve the user experience if you really know it. What is your need? What are your expectations? What are the pains he wants to alleviate when accessing your website or application? What does he really think about your product? What are your difficulties? All this is extremely important to define the next steps and priorities for your product.

Improve your content: When you know your target audience well, you can select the best arguments and choose the right moment to use them. In addition, you'll find out what content is needed to attract and convince users about the next steps or how to engage them in your product. This goes for every step, from the sales flow to lead generation and using the product itself.

Identify your best customers: Can you imagine that you might be wasting time and money trying to attract and convert people who simply aren't part of your ideal user profile? Therefore, knowing who they are, how they behave and where they are will significantly contribute to defining what you should offer in your product and how.

Adapt your UX for different profiles: Your site can be accessed by different user profiles, each with different expectations. If you don't know each one of them, you run the risk of creating a generic product that tries to serve everyone, but ends up serving no one effectively. Therefore, knowing and using personas can make your website or application two to five times more efficient and easier to use.

In summary, knowing your target audience is essential to the success of your product. By understanding users' needs, expectations and behaviors, you can target your development efforts, improve content, identify the best customers, and create a personalized and satisfying user experience. So don't underestimate the importance of knowing your user and let that guide your design and strategy decisions.

Grouping Users

Imagine that you have a product or service that is accessed by different people, each with unique characteristics. But somehow you realize that there are similarities between these people, allowing you to create personas to represent the most significant groups of users. How to do this?

First, you need to group users by common characteristics. Think about age group, gender, education level, occupation, what they do in real life, their goals when accessing your product and even the level of user experience. These are just a few examples of criteria that can be used to form groups. Based on this information, you will be ready to create personas.

Creating personas is simple but extremely valuable. Each persona needs to have a few essential elements:

Persona Name: Give your persona a name for easy identification and reference during product discussions. This will help you remember who she represents.

Age: Establish an age within the age range that best represents your users. This will help give the persona a more realistic context.

Education level: Find out what is the predominant education level among your users. This can range from elementary to higher education.

Occupation: Identify what is the most common occupation among your users. Do they work outside the home, hold management positions, are they housewives or students? This information is important to understand the context and needs of the persona.

Most used means of communication: Find out which are the main communication channels used by your users. This can include social networks, TV channels, electronic devices, among others.

Objectives: Understand the main objectives of the persona when using your product or service. Understanding individual goals and needs will help you create a more targeted experience.

Challenges: Identify the difficulties and pains that the persona faces. This allows you to understand specific needs and find suitable solutions.

How our company can help: This is the time to reflect on how your product or service can help overcome challenges and achieve the persona's goals. This is where you demonstrate the value your business offers.

Photo: Choose a photo that matches the description of the created persona. This will help you visualize it more realistically and make it easier to memorize its features.

Based on information about age, education, occupation, preferred means of communication and goals, you will be able to adapt the content, language and even the communication channels used to reach each persona more effectively.

By understanding each persona's specific challenges and pain points, you'll be able to offer better solutions. This will enable your company to position itself as a partner in the user's journey, helping them to overcome obstacles and achieve their goals.

Including a photo for each persona also plays an important role. It helps bring the fictional representation to life, making it more real and memorable. When you and your team can visualize the persona as a real person, it becomes easier to empathize and understand their needs in a deeper way.

Ultimately, personas become an essential tool for making decisions regarding the design, features, and priorities of your product or service. Based on the characteristics and preferences of the personas, you can direct your efforts to create a highly satisfactory user experience that meets the expectations and needs of each group.

taxonomy

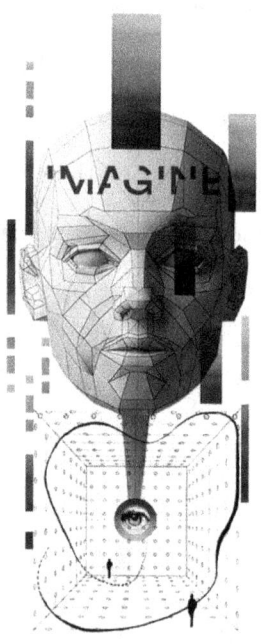

Taxonomy is a field of study dedicated to the classification and organization of elements or objects according to their characteristics and relationships.

Imagine that you are organizing a surprise party for a friend. To make sure everything is perfect and every detail is in the right place, you decide to apply the taxonomy.

First, you create general categories for easy organization. Let's say you have categories like decor, food, drink, music, and activities. These categories help group related elements into their respective areas.

Now, within the decor category, you create subcategories like balloons, banners, flower arrangements, and lighting. These subcategories allow for a more precise classification of the decorative elements you plan to use.

Under the food category, you can create subcategories such as appetizers, main courses, side dishes, and desserts. Each subcategory groups together the different types of food you plan to serve at the party.

Under the beverage category, you can have subcategories such as soft drinks, juices, alcoholic beverages, and water. These subcategories help organize the beverage options available to your guests.

In the music category, you can create subcategories such as party playlists, favorite birthday songs and dance songs. These subcategories let you select and organize songs according to the occasion.

Finally, under the activities category, you can have subcategories like games, pranks, and surprises. These subcategories help organize the different activities planned to entertain guests during the party.

By applying the taxonomy in this context, you can organize all the elements of the party in a logical and coherent way. This makes preparation easier, ensures nothing is forgotten, and helps create an enjoyable experience for the birthday person and guests.

As in the organization of the party, the taxonomy is a way of classifying and organizing elements according to their characteristics and relationships. It helps us create a logical structure and makes it easier to find and understand elements within a system.

This practice is widely used in many areas, such as biology, library science, computer science and information design.

In simple terms, taxonomy consists of grouping similar elements into categories or classes, in order to facilitate the understanding, search and retrieval of these elements. It involves creating a hierarchical classification system, in which elements are organized into levels of generality and specificity.

The taxonomy is based on specific criteria that are used to determine which category an element belongs to. These criteria can be based on physical characteristics, functional attributes, relationships between elements or any other aspect relevant to the classification. The goal is to create a consistent and intuitive system where each element is assigned to the most appropriate category.

One of the most common applications of taxonomy is in the organization of information and content. For example, on a website or in a digital library, taxonomy can be used to classify articles, pages or documents into specific categories and subcategories. This allows users to easily find the desired content by navigating through different rating levels.

In addition, taxonomy also plays an important role in creating efficient search systems. By assigning tags, keywords or metadata to elements, it is possible to improve the accuracy and relevance of search results, as elements are ranked according to their most relevant characteristics.

In the context of information design and user experience, taxonomy plays a key role in organizing and structuring information. It helps create more intuitive interfaces and makes it easier for users to find and understand information. A well-crafted taxonomy provides a more fluid and efficient user experience, allowing users to find what they are looking for quickly and intuitively.

In summary, by applying the taxonomy properly, it is possible to create clear and intuitive structures, making it easier for users to find and understand information.

5 problems in architecture

of the information

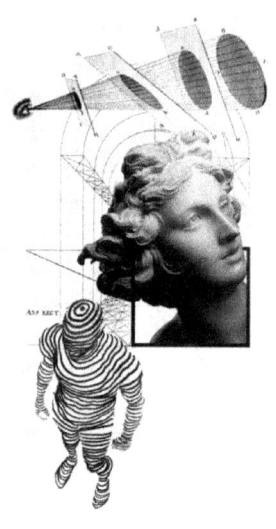

Information architecture plays a key role in creating intuitive and efficient digital experiences. It focuses on the organization, structure, and navigation of information within a product or system. However, even with careful planning, issues can arise that compromise usability and user experience. To identify these issues and ensure effective information architecture, here are 5 ways to spot them:

Metrics and Usage Data Analysis: An effective way to identify problems in the information architecture is to analyze product usage metrics and data. Through analysis tools, it is possible to identify user behavior patterns, such as bounce rates, time spent in certain sections and most common navigation paths. This information may reveal problematic points in the information structure, such as rarely accessed pages or difficulties in finding certain information.

Usability testing: Performing usability testing with real users is a valuable way to identify problems in information architecture. During testing, participants are asked to perform specific tasks on the product, while their interactions and difficulties are observed. Usability tests can reveal problems with confusing navigation, inadequate categorization of information, lack of clarity in the structure of the content, among other aspects that impact the user experience.

Heuristic evaluation: Heuristic evaluation is a technique in which UX experts analyze the product interface in search of usability issues. By applying a list of pre-defined heuristics, experts can identify common problems that affect information architecture, such as lack of consistency in the organization of information, lack of user feedback and lack of correspondence between the system and the real world. This approach offers a critical and objective view of the information structure.

Users' feedback: Users' opinion and feedback are invaluable in detecting problems in information architecture. Through surveys, interviews or support channels, it is possible to collect valuable information about the users' experience with the existing information structure. Users can report navigation difficulties, problems locating relevant information or suggestions for improving the organization of information. This direct user feedback can provide valuable insights to improve information architecture.

Competitor assessment and benchmarking: Observing and evaluating the information architecture of competing products or industry benchmarks can reveal interesting insights. By analyzing how other products organize their information and provide an efficient browsing experience, it is possible to identify potential gaps in the information architecture itself. This benchmarking approach can help identify opportunities for improvement and adapt best practices used in the market.

By using these 5 ways to detect problems in information architecture, you will be able to identify areas for improvement and take corrective actions to improve the user experience. It is important to remember that information architecture is not a static process, but rather a continuous cycle of analysis, tuning and optimization.

By analyzing usage metrics and data, performing usability tests, applying heuristic evaluations, collecting user feedback, and evaluating the competition, you will gain a comprehensive view of the effectiveness of your information architecture. These approaches complement each other, providing valuable insights and identifying potential problems in different aspects of the information structure.

Remember that early detection of information architecture issues is essential to avoid frustration and ensure a pleasant and intuitive user experience. By creating a cohesive, well-organized information structure, you'll be making it easy for users to find what they're looking for, navigate smoothly, and get to the relevant information quickly and efficiently.

Therefore, do not underestimate the importance of detecting and solving problems in the information architecture. Use these 5 forms of analytics and be constantly attentive to user needs and feedback. That way, you'll be on the right track to create digital products that offer an exceptional experience, adding value and achieving user satisfaction.

A/B Testing - The Variations of What Works

A/B testing is a fundamental strategy in the field of UX (User Experience) and digital marketing. It consists of presenting two different versions of a page, resource or element to users, and analyzing which one delivers better results in terms of engagement, conversions and user satisfaction.

The main advantage of A/B testing is that it allows you to make decisions based on hard data rather than assumptions or subjective opinions. By performing these tests, you can understand how small changes to the interface or content can have a significant impact on user behavior.

Here are some reasons why A/B testing is so important:

Continuous improvement: A/B testing enables constant improvement of the user experience. By running tests, you can identify what works best for your audience and adjust your strategy based on the results. This allows you to continually improve the usability, design and effectiveness of your product or website.

Conversion Optimization: The ultimate goal of any business is to convert visitors into customers or active users. A/B testing can help optimize conversion rates by identifying elements that encourage users to take desired actions, such as making a purchase, filling out a form, or signing up for a newsletter. By testing different variations, you can discover the most effective layout, text or calls-to-actions.

Risk reduction: Before implementing a significant change to a product or site, it is wise to test different approaches to reducing risk. A/B testing allows you to validate hypotheses and minimize the negative impact of wrong decisions. By testing small changes in a controlled way, you avoid rolling out big changes without being sure of their impact.

Experience personalization: Each user is unique and has different preferences and needs. A/B testing can help customize the user experience, offering variations tailored to different segments or user profiles. This may include changes to language, images, offers or content organization, allowing each user to have a more relevant and satisfying experience.

Evidence-based: When making decisions based on A/B testing, you have real data to back up your choices. This makes it easier to justify your decisions to the team or stakeholders, as you can show the positive impact of changes based on tangible results.

In summary, A/B testing is an essential tool to improve the user experience and optimize the results of a product or website. It lets you make informed decisions, reduce risk, personalize the experience, and constantly strive for continuous improvement. By implementing A/B testing into your strategy, you will be well on your way to delivering an exceptional user experience and achieving better results in your business goals.

Integrating texts into the design

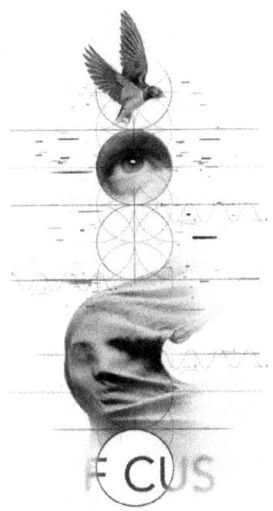

When you integrate text and design, you create an appropriate mix of visuals and textual content that can convey clear messages, provide relevant information, and grab the user's attention.

Let's explore some strategies for achieving that connection.

Visual coherence: Texts and images must be visually aligned, following the same design language, style and color palette. This helps create a cohesive and harmonious visual identity, conveying a unified message to users.

Content complementarity: The texts must complement the images, offering additional information or deepening the visual meaning. For example, on a travel website, an image of an exotic destination might be accompanied by text that describes local attractions, travel tips, and useful information.

Visual Hierarchy: Proper visual hierarchy allows users to easily identify the relationship between texts and images. Using font sizes, colors, and strategic placement can help highlight important information and direct the user's eye to relevant visual elements.

Contextualization: It is important to contextualize the images through descriptive texts or captions. This helps convey the purpose and meaning of the image, avoiding ambiguity and ensuring users understand the intended message.

Style Consistency: Maintain a consistent style throughout the design, both in text and images. This includes using consistent fonts, consistent writing styles, and images that fit the overall theme. Consistency helps create a unified and reliable experience.

Interaction: Explore ways of interacting between texts and images to engage users. For example, when hovering over an image, a description or additional related information may be displayed. This creates an interactive experience and increases user engagement.

Clarity and simplicity: Both texts and images must be clear and concise, avoiding excessive or complex information. Keep the message direct and to the point, ensuring that users can easily absorb the visual and textual content.

Understanding user needs and expectations is key to creating an effective and impactful combination. By balancing visual elements and textual content, you can provide a cohesive and meaningful experience, increasing usability and user satisfaction.

Intimacy with the real world

In the ever-evolving digital world, it is increasingly important to create experiences that bring users a sense of intimacy with the real world.

Although the internet and technology have given us access to a multitude of resources and possibilities, they can often seem impersonal and disconnected from our everyday reality.

However, by presenting the user with this intimacy with the real world, it is possible to create more authentic, engaging and memorable experiences.

One way to achieve this intimacy is through design and interaction.

By designing interfaces that resemble physical objects that users are familiar with, such as buttons that look like physical buttons, menus that mimic those in a restaurant, or visuals that hark back to real-world objects, we can create a sense of familiarity and comfort. .

This helps users feel more comfortable and makes it easier to understand and interact with the system.

Another approach is to use real-world elements to provide context and meaning.

For example, when presenting information or instructions, we may use metaphors or analogies related to the real world to make the content more understandable and relevant.

This allows users to connect with the information in a more meaningful way, relating it to experiences or concepts they already know.

In addition, we can exploit the power of personalization to create a sense of intimacy with the real world.

By allowing users to customize their settings, preferences and even the appearance of the interface, we are giving them the opportunity to create an environment that reflects their individual tastes and preferences.

This creates a sense of belonging and identification, bringing the digital experience closer to each user's personal reality.

Consider the sensory experience in creating an intimacy with the real world.

The incorporation of visual, sound and tactile elements can awaken emotions and memories associated with real experiences.

Familiar sounds, realistic animations, and even the tactile sensation when interacting with the interface can contribute to a more immersive and engaging experience.

By presenting the user with an intimacy with the real world, we are creating a deeper and more authentic connection. This results in a more engaging, memorable, and satisfying user experience.

By considering the user's context and expectations, using design elements, metaphors, personalization and sensory experience, we can create digital interfaces that transcend technology and become true extensions of the real world, enriching users' lives.

Agile UX

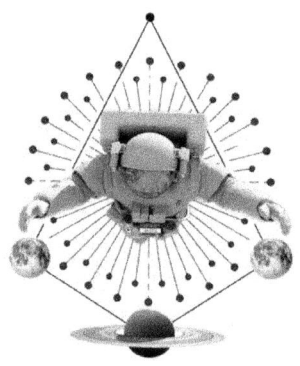

Agile UX is an approach that combines the principles of agile methodology with User Experience (UX) concepts and practices. This merger allows product and service development teams to create user experiences in a more collaborative, iterative, and user-centric way.

Agile methodology is known for its emphasis on flexibility, adaptation, and continuous delivery of customer value. She values frequent interaction between team members and being responsive to change during the development process. On the other hand, User Experience (UX) seeks to understand the needs, expectations and behaviors of users to design solutions that are useful, usable and enjoyable.

In the context of Agile UX, agile principles are applied to improve the way UX teams work. Rather than undertaking extensive research and detailed planning at the beginning of the project, Agile UX values continuous learning throughout the process. The UX team works closely with developers, business analysts and other members of the agile team to ensure user needs are met efficiently.

One of the key features of Agile UX is rapid, iterative prototyping. Rather than creating a complete design prior to development, the UX team produces low-fidelity prototypes that can be tested and refined with user feedback. This allows problems to be identified early and solutions to be iterated based on real evidence.

Another important aspect is multidisciplinary collaboration. Team members work together at every stage of the project, sharing knowledge and making joint decisions. This helps to avoid information silos and ensures that the user's view is considered in all decisions.

The Agile UX approach also emphasizes continuous value delivery. Rather than waiting until the end of the project to release the final product, Agile UX teams aim to deliver increments of user value in short intervals. This allows user feedback to be incorporated quickly and adjustments to be made throughout the development process.

In short, Agile UX combines agile principles with User Experience concepts to create a collaborative, iterative, and user-centric approach to product and service development. By incorporating rapid prototyping, cross-discipline collaboration, and continuous value delivery, Agile UX teams are more likely to create experiences that meet user needs and deliver effective results.

Lean UX - Lean thinking

Lean UX is an approach that combines lean thinking principles with User Experience (UX) concepts and practices. This methodology has the main objective of eliminating waste and maximizing the value delivered to the user, in an agile and efficient way.

Lean thinking, originating from the Japanese automobile industry, seeks to reduce all types of waste in a process, whether of time, resources or unnecessary efforts. In the context of Lean UX, this principle is applied to the development of products and services, with the aim of creating a more user-focused and results-oriented approach.

Unlike traditional UX approaches, which involve extensive research and detailed documentation, Lean UX values rapid experimentation and continuous learning. The idea is to test hypotheses and validate solutions iteratively, based on user feedback and real data.

One of the main characteristics of Lean UX is the emphasis on multidisciplinary collaboration. Teams are made up of members from different areas, such as design, development, business and marketing, who work together from the beginning of the project. This collaboration allows for a constant exchange of ideas and knowledge, resulting in solutions that are more integrated and in line with user needs.

Another fundamental aspect of Lean UX is the creation of MVPs (Minimum Viable Products) or MLPs (Minimum Loveable Products). These stripped-down versions of the product are rapidly developed and released to market for user feedback and validation. Based on these insights, the team can iterate and improve the product incrementally, avoiding wasting resources on unnecessary functionality.

The Lean UX approach also values the visualization of ideas and concepts. Instead of long documents or technical specifications, visual methods such as sketches, wireframes and storyboards are used to communicate and align the team's ideas. This helps to reduce ambiguity and speed up the development process.

Furthermore, Lean UX promotes the mindset of continuous experimentation and learning. Mistakes are seen as learning opportunities, and the team is always willing to adapt and adjust solutions based on the insights gained. This allows for constant product evolution, resulting in a more refined user experience aligned with the needs of the target audience.

In short, Lean UX is an agile and results-oriented approach that seeks to eliminate waste and maximize the value delivered to the user. With its emphasis on experimentation, multidisciplinary collaboration, and continuous learning, Lean UX offers an effective way to create products and services that are more in line with user needs, avoiding wasted resources and unnecessary effort.

Creating an MVP in practice

Creating an MVP (Minimum Viable Product) based on user experience using text and design involves following some important steps. Here are some guidelines to help with this process:

Define the objective: Start by clearly defining what the objective of your MVP is. Identify which user problem or need you want to solve and what value your product or service will deliver.

Identify the essential functionalities: Determine which are the main functionalities of your product that are necessary to fulfill the established objective. Focus on the minimum necessary to validate the value proposition and avoid developing unnecessary features.

Create a text structure: Develop a clear and concise text structure that will guide your MVP presentation. Organize the information logically, highlighting the main benefits and features of the product. Use direct and engaging language to convey the value proposition to users.

Design the interface: Use design to create an attractive and intuitive visual interface. Consider your brand's visual identity and create a clean, uncluttered layout. Prioritize usability by making user actions easy to understand and perform. Remember that the design must align with the product's value proposition.

Prototype user experience: Use prototyping tools to simulate user interaction with your MVP. This will allow you to test and validate the usability, navigability and fluidity of the user experience. Iterate on the prototype based on the feedback received, always looking to improve the interaction and understanding of the product.

Conduct usability tests: Invite representative users to test your MVP. Observe their interactions and collect feedback on the experience. Analyze metrics and identify areas for improvement. These tests will help validate text and design decisions, as well as identify potential issues or opportunities for improvement.

Make tweaks and iterations: Based on the usability test results, make any necessary tweaks to your MVP text and design. Iterate to refine the user experience, fix issues, and incorporate relevant feedback. This continuous improvement process is essential to create a product that is in line with the expectations and needs of users.

Remember that the purpose of the MVP is to validate the value proposition and gain learnings through interaction with users. So keep yourself open to tweaks and adaptations throughout the process. As you gather feedback and iterate, you'll get closer and closer to creating a meaningful and impactful user experience.

Users want transparency

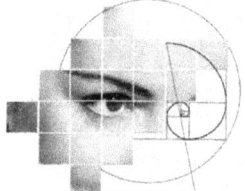

Users value transparency. There is no point in using small print with asterisks at the end of the screen, hiding the price, revealing the delivery time only at the end of the purchase or not making the exchange policy clear. It is essential that all this information is presented in a clear and accessible manner. Transparency is essential for the user to feel safe and confident when using your product.

When everything is laid out transparently, the user has a clear understanding of the conditions and expectations involved. This builds confidence, as he knows exactly what he is buying and what commitments he has made. In addition, transparency contributes to a healthy relationship between the company and the user, building a solid foundation of trust and loyalty.

In addition, it is important to avoid asking users for unnecessary data. Often, when faced with lengthy forms or excessive requests for personal information, users can feel uncomfortable and suspicious. So if you can simplify and minimize the amount of data requested, it will be even more favorable for the user experience.

Overall, by providing transparency and avoiding excessive solicitation of data, you demonstrate respect for the user and value their privacy. This makes for a more welcoming environment where users feel comfortable exploring and using your product. Transparency is a key factor in gaining user trust and cultivating a lasting relationship.

Large and obvious buttons

Did you know that a person's finger is, on average, 16-20mm? This information is essential when considering the size of clickable elements on your website or app.

When designing digital interfaces, it's crucial to ensure that users can easily interact with elements through touch. The size of click locations, also known as buttons or interactive areas, plays a key role in this regard.

By taking into account the average finger size, it is possible to prevent users from having difficulty hitting the desired target. If the click locations are too small, users may mistakenly tap adjacent areas, causing frustration and a negative experience.

On the other hand, by increasing the size of the click locations, you provide a more accurate and comfortable interaction. This means that users will be able to select the desired elements with greater ease and accuracy, reducing the chance of errors and improving the usability of your website or application.

In addition to size, it's also important to consider the spacing between click locations. It's a good idea to leave adequate space between interactive elements to prevent accidental touches and allow users to navigate easily.

When designing your interface, consider the average finger size of users and apply appropriate sizes to click locations. In this way, you will be creating a friendlier and more intuitive experience, making interaction with your website or application more pleasant and efficient for all users.

Conclusion

Throughout this material, we explore several aspects related to user experience (UX) and its importance in the creation of digital products.

We saw that UX involves the way users interact and perceive a product, considering factors such as usability, satisfaction and efficiency.

We discussed the fundamental pillars of usability, which are learning, efficiency, memorability, error prevention and user satisfaction.

These elements are essential to ensure a positive and pleasant experience for users, resulting in greater engagement and loyalty.

We also explore concepts such as taxonomy and information architecture, which play important roles in organizing and structuring information in a product.

The taxonomy helps in the categorization and organization of the contents, while the information architecture defines the way in which these contents are presented to the user.

We approach Nielsen's heuristics, a set of principles that help identify usability problems.

These heuristics provide important guidelines for creating more intuitive and efficient products, taking into account aspects such as feedback, consistency and flexibility.

We also talked about UX mindset, which involves adopting a user-centric mindset when designing and developing a product. Having a UX mindset means putting the user's needs and expectations at the forefront, constantly seeking to improve the experience offered.

Additionally, we explore agile approaches such as Agile UX and Lean UX that promote collaboration, iteration, and continuous adaptation during the development process.

These agile methodologies allow for a more flexible and efficient approach to building products based on user needs and feedback.

Finally, we emphasize the importance of A/B testing and MVP in the user experience. A/B testing allows you to compare two versions of an element or functionality to identify which offers a better user experience. The MVP (Minimum Viable Product) allows launching an initial version of the product with the minimum necessary functionalities, allowing testing and validating hypotheses based on user feedback.

In summary, user experience is a crucial factor in the development of successful digital products. Taking into account the principles of usability, adopting a user-centric mindset, using agile approaches, and performing constant tests and interactions are fundamental practices to create products that meet the needs and expectations of users, providing a positive, efficient, and memorable experience.

Who is Matheus Martins Soares?

Matheus is an Ex-Military / Presidential Agent, graduated in Marketing since 2018 and specialist in copywriting. He has written for more than 27 different niches, showing his ability to adapt to different topics and audiences. Throughout his career, he has worked in large companies, such as the largest business magazine in the country and the largest marketing consultancy in Brazil. Contributed to the success of important campaigns, generating + 30m in sales for its customers. Published over 200 books on Amazon and gained readers in over 12 different countries. An expert in StoryTelling and UX Writing, he also works behind the scenes as a GhostWriter, giving voice to other people's ideas and stories. His method is capable of writing a book in less than 24 hours.

With a strategic vision and knowledge in marketing, he helps companies, authors and literary projects to achieve success. He found himself in the world of marketing, writing and human behavior.

www.ingramcontent.com/pod-product-compliance
Lightning Source LLC
Chambersburg PA
CBHW052332220526
45472CB00001B/380